Magic

Unlock the secrets of magic tricks
& become a master of illusion

Barb Whiter

MUD PUDDLE BOOKS, INC.
New York, New York

Magic:
Unlock the secrets of magic tricks
& become a master of illusion

Written by Barb Whiter

Published by
Mud Puddle Books, Inc.
54 W. 21st Street
Suite 601
New York, NY 10010

info@mudpuddlebooks.com

Originally published by
Hinkler Books Pty Ltd
17-23 Redwood Drive
Dingley, Victoria 3172 Australia
www.hinklerbooks.com

Illustrations by Monitor Graphics Pty Ltd

ISBN: 1-59412-073-0

Printed and bound in China

3. Throw the dice and insist on silence while you concentrate on the numbers (diagram 1). Wave your hand or a magic wand over the dice (diagram 2), then show the underside of each one to the audience, saying the number as you do so. So, if three was showing, as you pick up the dice shout "Four"— and you'll be right.

diagram 2

Dicey Numbers

This is a simple trick which relies on a mathematical certainty—the opposite sides of a dice always add up to seven!   Remember this, and the trick will make you look so-o-o-o-o good!

You need: three dice

1.   Hand the dice around the audience so they can see the dice are not trick dice.

2.   Tell the audience how you can see through the dice and can read the number underneath each one—because of trained mental powers! (Remember, seven is the total!)

diagram 1

Contents

Introduction: Where Do I Begin? • • • • • • • • 5

Putting a Show Together • • • • • • • • • • 7

Performing for a Real Audience • • • • • • • • 9

THE TRICKS!

How Many Balls? • • • • • • • • • • • • • • 11

Eleven Fingers • • • • • • • • • • • • • • • 13

Linking Rings • • • • • • • • • • • • • • • 15

Rings of Magic • • • • • • • • • • • • • • • 17

Rubber Band Escape • • • • • • • • • • • • 19

Obedient Ice Cube • • • • • • • • • • • • • 21

The Unbreakable Match • • • • • • • • • • • 23

The Magnetic Wand • • • • • • • • • • • • 25

Bits and Pieces • • • • • • • • • • • • • • • 27

The Vanishing Knot • • • • • • • • • • • • • **29**

The Self-Tying Handkerchief • • • • • • • • **31**

The Hypnotized Handkerchief • • • • • • • **33**

How Eggstraordinary! • • • • • • • • • • **35**

Magic Card Twist • • • • • • • • • • • • **37**

Sticky Hands • • • • • • • • • • • • • • • • **39**

Choose a Card, Any Card • • • • • • • • **41**

Find the Card • • • • • • • • • • • • • • • **43**

The Mysterious Balancing Coin • • • • • **45**

Gone! Into Thin Air • • • • • • • • • • • • **47**

Where's That Coin? • • • • • • • • • • • • **49**

"Now You See It, Now You Don't" • • • • • **51**

Seeing Double—Or None? • • • • • • • • • **53**

The Knot Challenge • • • • • • • • • • • **56**

Making Money • • • • • • • • • • • • • • • **57**

Fruit or Vegetable • • • • • • • • • • • • **59**

Hocus Pocus • • • • • • • • • • • • • • • **61**

Dicey Numbers • • • • • • • • • • • • • • **63**

Introduction
Where Do I Begin?

It's easy to learn to be an expert magician with the tips and step-by-step instructions found in this magic book for beginners. Even those who have had some practice in the magic arts could find a trick or two worthy of them in this book.

Here are a few tips:

✔ Set aside an hour to practice your tricks and do it regularly, say three times every week. Treat magic like you do your homework, but remember to have fun!

✔ Don't perform a trick in public until you are confident of being able to perform while doing the following:

- have one hand behind your back,
- wear a blindfold and perform without having to think about what you are doing.

✔ It's hard to accomplish the above; however, you will find if you spend time learning the tricks properly, your audience will really appreciate your performance.

✔ Also, working out what you are going to say in advance will enhance the audience's experience. Maybe write it down first, then learn it by heart before performing the trick—timing is everything!

✔ Never ever tell anyone how you do your tricks. This totally ruins the effect of the trick, plus it takes the shine off your performance completely. Sometimes it's tempting to tell, but don't!

✔ Practice in front of a mirror so you can see exactly what your audience sees. Or get a family member to video you as you perform or practice as this will enable you to see where you can improve.

✔ Learn to do tricks perfectly. Near enough is not good enough in magic! Five tricks done perfectly are much more fun to watch than ten done poorly—and they're much more fun to perform too!

✔ Don't start practicing another trick until you've accomplished the one before!

Putting a Show Together

Once you have an accomplished performance of about 10 to 12 tricks, then it's time to put on a little show! Start off with a show which lasts for about 20 minutes. Once this feels good, increase the length of the performance to around 30 minutes, adding more tricks.

A successful show has a beginning, a middle and an end. Always start off with a warm-up, which is short but has a startling effect on your audience. When creating your routine try not to put two similar effects together, or two long or two short tricks right next to each other; try to mix them up.

Although we've put several coin or card tricks together in the book, learn them all, but mix the performance of them up when planning your act.

Obviously, you'll need to time each trick you learn and then you'll proba-bly have to try your routine out a couple of times to get the best

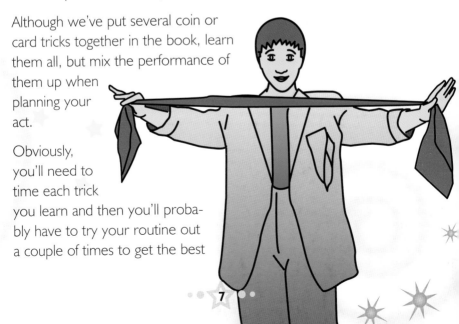

flow of tricks going. It's a great idea to ask mom or dad to give you a hand with this. They can watch and give you advice at the end or, even better, if you have a video camera or they could borrow one, they could video your performance and you can then watch it together to see where it needs some improvement.

Pace yourself—when you are talking to your audience, don't talk quickly—and remember variety is the spice of a good magic show.

Shazam!

Performing for a Real Audience

It doesn't matter if your first real audience is just a couple of your best friends, it can still be hard. You'll probably get butterflies in your stomach, sweaty palms, and you could even stutter or stammer out your lines, even if you've never stuttered or stammered in your life before!

This is called "stage fright" but, don't worry, it happens to everybody. Just take your time, breathe deeply and start off slowly with the trick you know best!

A good idea is to do small shows for your family and a couple of friends, and maybe even run through it a few times. This should get your confidence booming and you can then fine-tune any areas which need it.

Remember, each audience is different, so you may have to change the routine a little bit to cater for this. As you increase your level of performance, you'll find you will be able to gauge your audiences better and provide just the right level of performance for them.

You may also have audiences of different age groups—younger kids one day and older the next. For the younger kids, your best bet is to do fewer tricks than you thought you would, and keep them simple and easy to see. Remember, younger kids are usually shorter and won't be able to see you as well if you stand up tall and talk and perform over their heads.

Hey, most of all, though—have fun!!!

How Many Balls?

You need: three small, soft balls

Palming an object: Before doing this trick, practice "palming" a ball. To palm an object means to hide it in your palm so the audience doesn't know it's there.

To begin, put a ball in the palm of your hand and close your thumb slightly so the ball is held in place and gripped by the muscle at the base of your thumb. Practice with both hands until you can hold the ball like this and move your hands about at the same time. Keep practicing until you are good enough to palm two balls comfortably in the one hand.

1. Start by palming one ball in your left hand. Now pick up the other two balls with your right hand and show them to the audience.

2. Ask for a volunteer from the audience. Ask them to hold out their hands and place one ball in each hand.

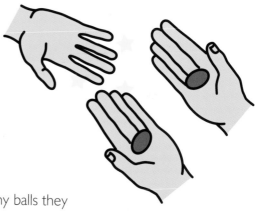

3. Ask them how many balls they have. When they say "Two", reach over towards them, smile and pull another one out from behind their ear—with your left hand.

How it's done: The third ball (the one you palmed) was in your left hand all the time of course, your audience doesn't know this! As you bring your hand back from near the volunteer's ear, you release the ball, to more applause.

Eleven Fingers

This trick can be performed by anyone! It's good to begin a perform-ance with as it relies on no props—just you keeping the audience interested.

You need: ten fingers

1. Tell your friends you have eleven fingers and you can prove it. Using your right forefinger to point with, touch each finger of your left hand, counting "One, two, three, four, five."

2. Then, with your left forefinger, count the fingers on your right hand, "Six, seven, eight, nine, ten." Say, "I know I had eleven fingers this morning! Let's try again."

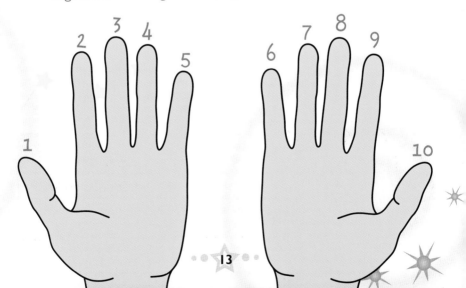

3. This time, count backwards, pointing to the fingers as you say, "Ten, nine, eight, seven, six."

4. Then stop, hold up the right hand and say, "Plus five equals eleven!" Do this quickly and without pausing.

Linking
Rings

As this is a simple trick, you'll need some good "patter" to entertain the audience while you conduct the trick. Perhaps talk about the secret magic spell you need to weave—make up your own to say out loud.

You need: three linking rings—one has a split—and a magic wand

1.   Hold all three rings and hide the opening in the split ring with your fingers.

2. Bring all three rings together, tap them with your magic wand while chanting your spell.

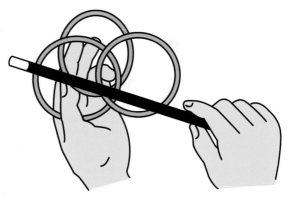

3. Show the audience all three rings linked together.

How it's done: When you bring the rings together, slip the two solid rings through the open part of the split one, so they link. This will need practice so you can do it with one hand while tapping the wand on the rings with the other.

Rings of Magic

Another simple trick which relies on planning and lots of practice.

You need: piece of rope, two rings

1. Show the rope and one ring to the audience. In fact, let them examine them to see there are no tricks here—this is magic!

2. Ask someone to tie the rope around your wrists as shown in the diagram.

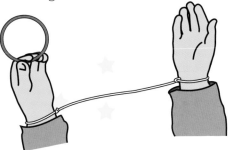

3. Turn away briefly, while saying a magic spell so the audience is entertained, and then turn back to show the ring threaded onto the rope!

How it's done: Before beginning, hide a similar ring up your sleeve. Then when you turn around to say your spell, slip the first ring into your pocket and slide the hidden ring down your arm and along the rope.

Rubber Band
Escape

How to make a rubber band jump from your first two fingers to your second two fingers. It looks impressive when done smoothly.

You need: one medium-sized rubber band

1. Place a rubber band over your forefinger and middle finger (diagram 1). Bring the rubber band down to the base of your fingers. Hold your hand so its back is facing the audience.

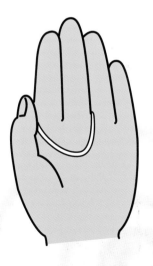

2. Pull the rubber band with your other hand to show that it is solid, then curl your fingers down and under the rubber band (diagram 2). From the audience's view it looks like the rubber band is still around only two of your fingers.

3. Pause for an instant, then straighten your fingers out. The band will instantly jump over to your ring finger and pinky (diagram 3).

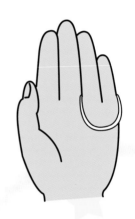

4. To make the rubber band jump back to your first two fingers, follow exactly the same moves. Hey presto! The rubber band is back on the original two fingers.

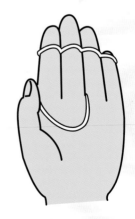

Obedient
Ice Cube

You can lift an ice cube without touching it, but because this trick can take a few seconds to work, you will need a good line in "patter" to keep your audience's attention.

You need: ice cube, glass, water, string, salt

1. Put the ice cube into the glass of water.

2. Place one end of the string on top of the ice cube. At this point you can get some of the audience to try to lift up the ice cube.

3. Pour some salt onto the ice cube and string. It is best to wait a few seconds and then lift the string up.

SALT

4. Wow! The ice cube will stick to the string and can be lifted from the glass.

Hocus Pocus

The Unbreakable Match

Place a match in a handkerchief, wrap it up and break it, then—
abracadabra!—it's whole again.

You need: one handkerchief with a hem, one match (to hide in
the hem of the handkerchief), several extra matches as props

1. Before facing your audience, conceal a match in the hem of
the handkerchief. Display the handkerchief and several other
matches.

2. Ask a volunteer to point to one of the matches and then pick
up the match they choose. Place
it in the center of the
handkerchief and roll
the handkerchief up
with the chosen match
in its center.

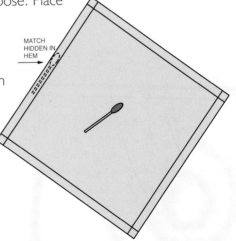

MATCH
HIDDEN IN
HEM

3. While doing this, take hold of the match already concealed in the hem of the handkerchief and hand this to the volunteer. Ask them to confirm to the rest of the audience they can feel the match through the handkerchief. Invite them to break it in half!

4. Take the handkerchief back and break the hidden match again! Everyone will think the match which has been broken is the same one they saw you roll up in the handkerchief a few moments earlier. Now, slowly unroll the handkerchief and show the match—unbroken—in fact, completely whole!

The Magnetic Wand

This is probably the easiest trick you could ever come across, but it is very effective when done with a little practice and a touch of magic!

You need: a magic wand

1. Clasp the wand in your left hand (diagram 1).

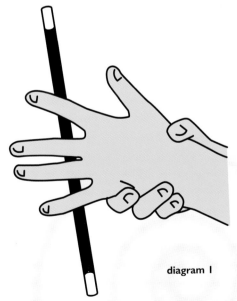

diagram 1

2. Hold your left wrist with your right hand, keeping the wand in place with your right index finger (diagram 2).

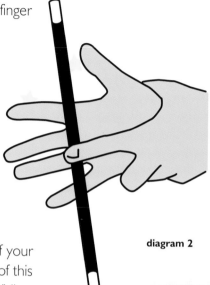

diagram 2

3. Slowly unclasp the fingers of your left hand, keeping the back of this hand facing the audience. While doing this you need to be talking to the audience and saying a magnetic spell!

4. Slide the wand down your palm a little then clasp your fingers again and remove your right hand. Wow!!

Bits and Pieces

A piece of string or thin rope is cut into two and then magically restored to one piece with just a touch of magic!

You need: one piece of string or thin rope, a piece of writing paper, a pair of sharp scissors—be careful!

1. Fold a piece of paper before the show so it looks like the paper in diagram 1. Fold the top of the paper (A) down, then fold the bottom of the paper (C) up. When it is time to do your trick, pull out the paper and lay the string in it as shown.

diagram 1

2. Now for the secret move. When you fold C over A, use your thumb to catch the string as shown in diagram 2. Note: when you fold the paper before the show, make sure A is not long enough to cover the string.

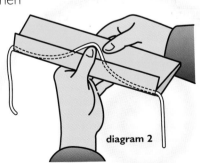

diagram 2

3. Securely grasp the paper and string as shown in diagram 3, making sure the view shown is only seen by you.

4. Cut through the paper and, presumably, cut the string in half (diagram 4). In reality, only the paper is cut in half and the string is completely untouched.

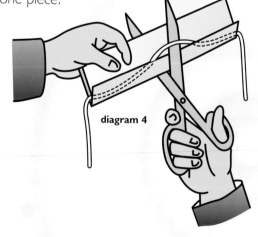

diagram 3

5. To complete the trick, crumple up the paper with a flourish and pull the rope out slowly. Show your audience it is restored to one piece.

Encourage your audience to examine the paper, and they will see that it has been cleanly cut into two halves.

diagram 4

The Vanishing Knot

How to make a knot disappear from a rope or handkerchief!

You need: a handkerchief, small scarf or a piece of soft rope

1. First, twirl the handkerchief or scarf into a ropelike shape. Hold it slightly apart between the index and middle fingers of each hand, keeping your palms up (diagram 1).

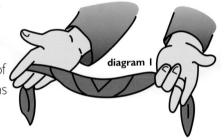

diagram 1

2. Take the ends in your right hand and place between the thumb and forefinger of the left hand (diagram 2).

diagram 2

3. You are still holding onto part of the handkerchief with your right hand. Use your right hand to position the part of the handkerchief between the second and third fingers of your left hand, as you reach through the loop with your right hand and grasp the closest dangling end (diagram 3).

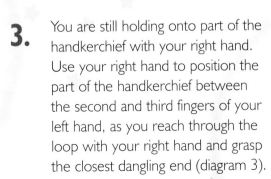

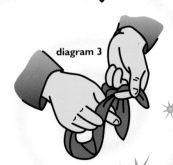

diagram 3

4. Pull that end through the loop, keeping a grip on the handkerchief between the second and third fingers (diagram 4). Pull the end through with your right hand. You will notice a loop forms around your left middle finger. Withdraw your finger, leaving the loop hidden behind the knot and display the hanging knot (diagram 5).

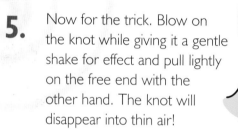

diagram 4

5. Now for the trick. Blow on the knot while giving it a gentle shake for effect and pull lightly on the free end with the other hand. The knot will disappear into thin air!

diagram 5

6. Great applause!

The Self-Tying Handkerchief

A knot instantly ties itself at the end of a handkerchief in this trick, which relies on good "patter" to entertain the audience and a flowing execution of what is a really simple, effective trick.

You need: a handkerchief with a knot tied in one corner

1. Tell your friends you can tie a knot in a handkerchief using only one hand. Pull the handkerchief from your pocket, but keep the knot hidden (diagram 1).

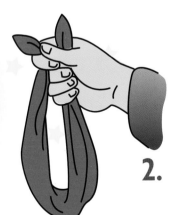

2. Pick up the opposite corner of the handkerchief with the other hand and grasp it (diagram 2).

3. Snap the handkerchief, releasing the end without the knot (diagram 3). Pick up the hanging end with the other hand as before and repeat, again releasing the end without the knot.

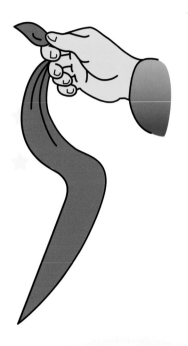

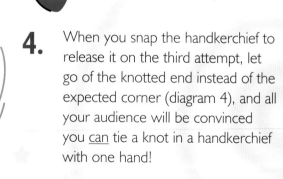

4. When you snap the handkerchief to release it on the third attempt, let go of the knotted end instead of the expected corner (diagram 4), and all your audience will be convinced you <u>can</u> tie a knot in a handkerchief with one hand!

The Hypnotized Handkerchief

You can begin this trick by telling your audience you've spent hours training a handkerchief under hypnosis to follow your every wish!

You need: one handkerchief with a hem, a pipe-cleaner or a drinking straw

1. Prepare this trick by threading the pipe-cleaner (or a flattened straw) into the hem of the handkerchief as shown in diagram 1. Make certain the pipe-cleaner is secured in place so it won't slip down in the hem. You may need to sew a few threads in place across the hem to make sure.

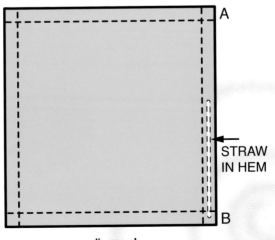

A

STRAW
IN HEM

B

diagram 1

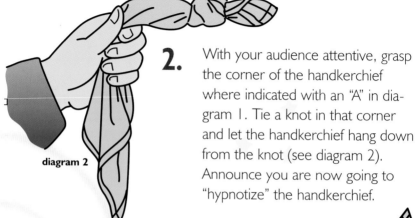

diagram 2

2. With your audience attentive, grasp the corner of the handkerchief where indicated with an "A" in diagram 1. Tie a knot in that corner and let the handkerchief hang down from the knot (see diagram 2). Announce you are now going to "hypnotize" the handkerchief.

3. With the other hand, take the middle of the handkerchief where corner "B" is in diagram 1 and drop the knot. Gesture with your free hand as if "hypnotizing the handkerchief." By gently moving your thumb on the base of the pipe-cleaner, you can cause the handkerchief to slowly rise until it seems balanced on your fingers. For an even better effect, you can then gently let the handkerchief drop back down.

diagram 3

4. For an impressive finale, throw the handkerchief up high above your head, catch it and crumple it into a ball and take a bow!

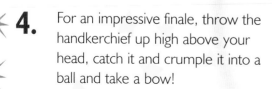

How Eggstraordinary!

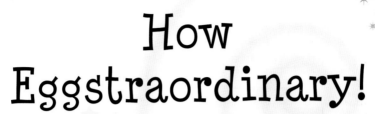

Done well, with lots of clever chat, your astounded audience will believe you can pull a handkerchief out of an egg.

You need: an egg, a small silk handkerchief, a teaspoon, an egg cup (optional)

1. First, prepare the egg for your show. Make a hole on the side of an uncooked egg. Gently spoon out the contents of the egg (have scrambled eggs for tea!). Wash the shell inside and let it sit and dry naturally. Remember to be careful while doing this. Once the shell has dried, carefully poke your silk hanky into the hole with a pencil—see diagram 1.

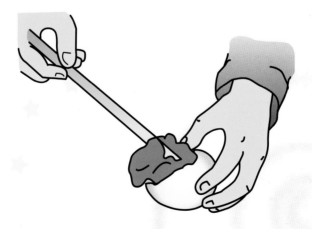

2. Now, the clever thing is to convince your audience you have lost your hanky, but you're going to eat an egg instead. Of course, they will think it's a boiled egg so, when you hold it up in the air for the audience to see, keeping the hole towards you, you could pretend it's hot if you like— see diagram 2.

3. Now, pop it back on the table and tap it gently with your spoon, then gasp and say something like "How eggstraordinary! You'll never guess where I've found my hanky" (diagram 3).

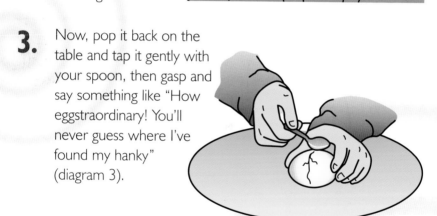

4. Break the egg apart excitedly and pull out the hanky, waving it in the air as in diagram 4.

Magic Card Twist

To fool the audience with this trick, you will need to practice to get it right.

You need: white cardboard, red and black felt-tip pens

1. Again, preparation is important; you need to create the magic card first! Just cut out a piece of white cardboard approx. 2 inches wide x 3.5 inches high (54mm wide x 88mm high). On one side color in five red dots and the other side two black dots (diagram 1).

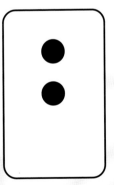

2. Hold the card up for the audience to see and say this card has six dots. Place your finger on the blank area (diagram 2). Then turn the card over and say now it only has one dot. Again, place your finger over one of the black dots (diagram 3).

3. Turn the card over again and say, "Wow! Now there are only four spots!". Use your finger to cover the middle red dot (diagram 4).

4. Then, turn the card again and exclaim, "Gosh, now there are three black dots. This card has four sides!". Use your finger at the end of the card where there is no black dot to suggest there is one missing under your finger!

Sticky Hands

Just use magic to make sure these cards "stick" to your hand without any glue.

You need: playing cards, a ring, a toothpick

1. Before facing your audience, place the ring on your middle finger if possible. If it won't fit, your ring finger will be okay. Now slide the toothpick under the ring (diagram 1).

2. Place your hand palm-down on top of your table, so the audience can only see the back of your hand. Be careful as you don't want anyone seeing the toothpick underneath. Tell the audience how you can magically hold several cards at a time, without the aid of anything but your magical powers.

diagram 1

3. With your free hand, take a playing card and slide it under the hand on the table, making sure it also slides under one end of the toothpick (diagram 2).

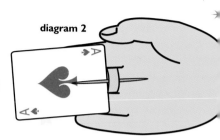

diagram 2

4. Take another card and slide it under your hand, putting it between your hand and the other end of the toothpick (diagram 3).

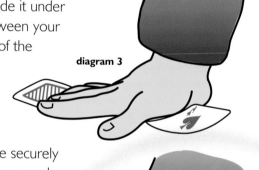

diagram 3

5. Once these two cards are securely in place, they will hold more cards. Slide some extra cards under your hand just to make it look really good (diagram 4).

diagram 4

6. Slowly lift your hand from the table while saying your favorite magic word, such as "Alicazam!" The cards will "stick" to the palm of your hand —it's magic!

Choose a Card, Any Card!

That's what you can say to your audience volunteer for this simple but effective card trick to work well every time you use it. It's a really good trick to begin a show because it's quick and shows you know your stuff!

You need: a pack of cards

1. The only thing you need to do before beginning this trick is to shuffle the cards and memorize the bottom card. Later in the trick when you ask the volunteer to cut the cards, the card they chose will be the card below the bottom card you've remembered, so you'll be able to be right every time.

diagram 1

2. So you've shuffled the cards and memorized the bottom card, now offer the pack fanned out as in diagram 1 to a member of the audience and ask them to pick one card, look at it and memorize it without letting you see or hear what it is.

3. Ask them to place the card face down on top of the pack and then ask them to cut the cards once. This means they divide the pack into two wherever they want to. Then move the top section to the bottom of the pack as in diagram 2.

diagram 2

4. Deal out the cards one at a time slowly and methodically, even taking some time to stare at one or two cards as if they may be the right ones—it's part of a performance after all— then stop at the correct card (diagram 3). Everyone will be impressed!

diagram 3

42

Find the Card

Another easy card trick which looks impressive, after a little bit of organizing on your part.

You need: a deck of "marked" cards, fine-line markers, one red & one black

1. To prepare for this trick you will first need to mark a pack of cards. To do this just get a black marker and put a small dot on the upper left hand corner above the number or symbol of all the black cards. Then get the red marker and do the same thing for the red cards. Check every card has a small dot.

2. Now fan out the cards and let an audience member pick a card. Ask the person to look at it and memorize it.

3. While the audience member is looking at the card, secretly turn the deck around in your hand and fan them out again (diagram 2).

4. Ask the audience member to put the card back into the deck of cards. Make sure its marking is facing the opposite way. Shuffle the deck of cards, being careful to keep the cards facing in the same direction.

5. Fan through the deck of cards until you find which card is turned around. You'll need to use your fingers and seem to be getting inspired by your magic powers to find this tricky card. Hold up the card and ask the audience member, "Is this the card you picked?" It will be.

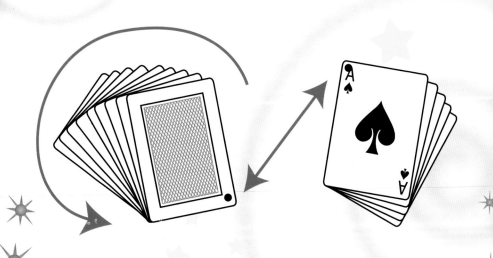

The Mysterious
Balancing Coin

You can balance a coin on your fingertips, but no-one else can!

You need: one large coin, one straight pin

1. The trick here is some preparation. Before you start, conceal a straight pin in one hand between the first two fingers.

2. With the other hand, pull a coin out of your pocket and allow it to be examined by the audience. When you get the coin back, lay it down on top of the straight pin in your other hand.

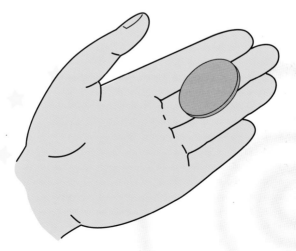

3. Now raise the coin to a standing position near the ends of your fingers and, as you do, raise the straight pin with it, making sure no one knows the pin is there. Keep pressure on the pin and the coin will balance there as if held by unseen forces!

4. After a few moments, slowly release pressure on the pin. This should let the coin gently drift back down onto your fingers! Don't forget to get rid of the pin while the audience is examining the coin.

5. This is a simple trick which needs lots of practice to get the pressure on the pin correct. It's worth it!

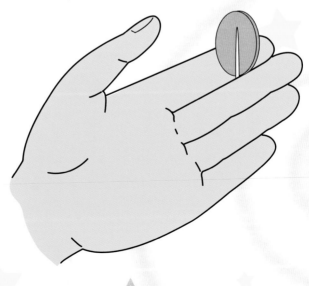

Gone! Into Thin Air

So you've dazzled the audience with finding the cards they picked, but how about making cards disappear?   That would be fun ...

You need: a pack of cards, handkerchief with a hem, toothpick, scissors

1. A little preparation for this trick is necessary. Make sure the toothpick is as long as the width of a playing card—if it's too long, trim it. Now poke this toothpick into the hem of the handkerchief—diagram 1. You're ready for an audience!

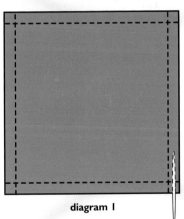

diagram 1

2. Begin with a flourish by spreading the deck of cards on your show table. Wave the handkerchief about and tell your audience you'll pick a card from the deck and make it vanish into thin air.

3. Lay the handkerchief over the card so the edge with the toothpick faces away from the audience—diagram 2.

diagram 2

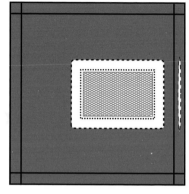

diagram 3

4. Pick up the edge of the handkerchief which contains the toothpick by holding the toothpick between your thumb and index finger. It looks as if you are holding a playing card—right? (diagram 3).

5. Say your favorite magic words, including something about making the card disappear. Throw the handkerchief into the air—the card appears to have vanished!

Where's That Coin?

A coin is placed in the center of a handkerchief in full view of an audience—the magician weaves a magic spell—and it's gone!

You need: a handkerchief, a coin, BluTack (or similar reusable adhesive)

1. Before facing your audience, stick a small piece of BluTack on one corner of the handkerchief. This needs to be kept hidden from the audience at all times during the performance.

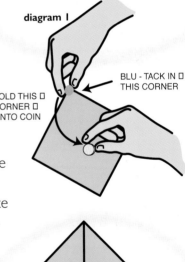

diagram 1

BLU - TACK IN □ THIS CORNER

FOLD THIS □ CORNER □ ONTO COIN

2. Spread the handkerchief out on the show table, keeping hold of the corner which has the BluTack. Place the coin in the center of the hand-kerchief and immediately cover it with the corner with the BluTack as in diagram 1.

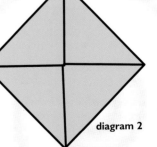

3. Fold the other three corners into the center of the handkerchief over the coin as in diagram 2.

diagram 2

4. Place the fingers of both your hands under the folded edge of the handkerchief which is nearest you—diagram 3. Because of this quick move, the coin, stuck to the handkerchief, ends up in your hand.

diagram 3

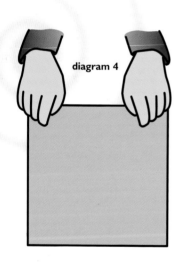

diagram 4

5. Show both sides of the handkerchief with a flourish to the audience, give it a quick shake and put it in your pocket to finish. Alternatively, pretend to blow your nose on it, or pretend to sneeze and cover your nose and mouth with it—anything for a finale and a good round of applause!

Perhaps you would like to make this coin reappear? It can be done—of course it can—it's magic! Or it's good planning. Simply have an identical coin hidden somewhere strange—down the top of your sock maybe, or when you remove the coin from the handkerchief keep it in your hand and then produce it from anywhere you like. Perhaps from behind the ear of one of your audience members?

" Now You See It, Now You Don't "

Actually the saying needs to be reversed for this disappearing and reappearing coin. Read on!

You need: two sheets of the same colored paper, one is used to disguise the rim of the glass and the other is the sheet underneath on which the magic is displayed; one sheet of paper in another color for the cone; glass; glue, scissors; coin

1. Make the magic cone first by rolling the colored paper as shown in diagram 1. Glue it in place and add stars and glitter to give it extra magic powers.

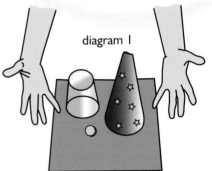

diagram 1

2. Next, cut out a circle of the other colored paper using the glass as your guide and glue it to the rim of the glass. This will cover the coin and be camouflaged because it will be resting on paper of the same color—diagram 2. Now you're ready to proceed.

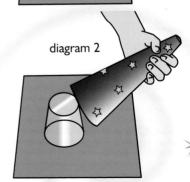

diagram 2

3. You have the magic cone, glass and coin resting on the colored paper. Tell your audience the cone is endowed with magic powers and can make things disappear. You will make the coin disappear.

4. Cover the glass with the cone and place it over the coin. Tap the cone with a wand or simply wave your hands about saying magic words, such as "Abracadabra!"—diagram 3.

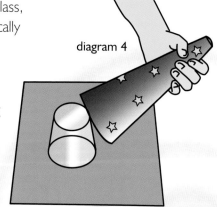

diagram 3

5. Lift up the cone to show the glass, but no coin—it has been magically spirited away—diagram 4.

diagram 4

6. Of course, the coin is still sitting on the table, but because the same colored paper covers the rim of the glass, it appears the coin has gone.

7. Therefore, it's so easy for you to become the really clever magician and restore the coin to the table by reversing the process. Place the cone over the glass again, say a few simple magic words with a flourish of hands, and pick up the cone and the glass, and there it is—the coin has reappeared!

Seeing Double— or None?

You need: a small paper bag, a coin, two identical playing cards

1. To get ready for this trick, place one of the identical playing cards in the bottom of the paper bag. Now scrunch the top of the bag (diagram 1).

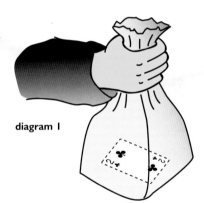

diagram 1

2. Put the paper bag, the other playing card and the coin on your table and tell the audience that you have one coin and one playing card (diagram 2).

diagram 2

3. Put the playing card and coin into the bag slowly and deliberately just to show the audience exactly what has gone into the bag.

4. Now squeeze the bag shut and shake it up and down. You might want to pass it onto a few audience members to shake, but don't let them look inside. Wave your magic wand over the bag (diagram 3).

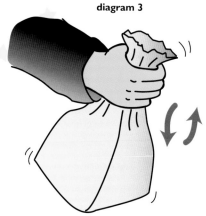

diagram 3

5. Open the bag and reach into it. Now carefully take the card out of the bag and also take the coin out at the same time, so no one in the audience sees it. To do this, you hide the coin behind the playing card, only showing the audience the playing card as it comes out (diagram 4).

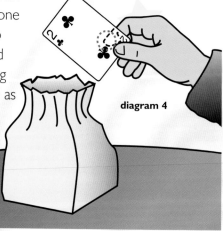

diagram 4

6. Drop both the card and coin into your pocket.

7. Ask an audience member what they think will be in the bag. Of course, they will say "a coin," but, hey presto, you pull another playing card out of the bag in its place! Or, to make more of an impact, ask an audience member, "What's left in my bag now?" They'll say, "a coin," so get them up to pull out whatever's in the bag—the other playing card (diagram 5).

Hey-Presto

diagram 5

The Knot Challenge

Challenge your friends to tie a knot in a piece of rope without letting go of the ends. Unless they've seen the trick before, none of them will be able to do it.

You need: a piece of rope about three feet (one meter) long

1. This is an easy one, but it only works once! Show your friends how to hold the rope as in the diagram, and then let them try to tie a knot in the rope without letting go of either end at any time.

2. When they give up, as they soon will, take back the rope and place it on a table.

3. Now you can do this trick because you know the secret move. Just fold your arms across you chest before you pick up the rope, one end at a time. When you unfold your arms, a knot will appear in the middle of the rope and you won't have let go of either end. What a genius!

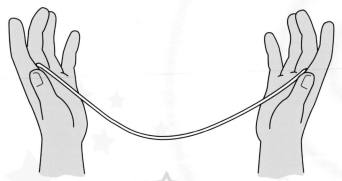

Making Money

A great trick to show just how easy it is to make money!

You need: two similar coins, an empty matchbox with a sliding drawer

1. Before the audience is admitted to the show, you have to open the matchbox halfway and wedge one of the coins between the back edge of the drawer and the top of the box (diagram 1). Put the other coin in your pocket.

diagram 1

2. Show the half-opened matchbox to your audience and encourage an audience member to have a look inside the matchbox, but don't let them hold it.

3. Ask if someone in the audience has a coin you could borrow for this trick. Use this coin as the second coin during the trick. If no one has a coin, then you have the spare one in your pocket.

4. Put the coin into the matchbox and ask someone different in the audience to see that it is in the matchbox. Just remember, don't let anyone hold the box (diagram 2).

diagram 2

5. Close the matchbox drawer. When you do this, the other coin, which is wedged in at the top, will drop down into the drawer.

6. Now's the time to really put in a performance! Much waving of hands, or use of a wand, and lots of magic words or spells are needed now. And then, open the matchbox drawer with a flourish—there are two coins nestled there (diagram 3).

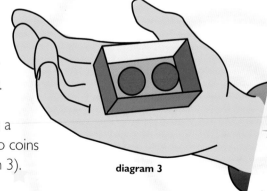

diagram 3

Fruit or Vegetable?

Sometimes the simplest tricks are the best. Well, this is one of the best!

You need: a sheet of paper, three pencils and a hat

1. Prepare for the trick before your audience arrives by tearing a sheet of paper into three equal portions. The trick here is in the tearing-you need to be able to feel the uneven edges of the pieces of paper to enable you to complete the trick. So don't use scissors!

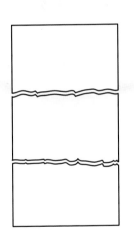

2. Once the audience arrives, ask for three volunteers to come forward to help you with the trick. Hand two volunteers pieces of paper with only one torn edge, that is a piece taken from the end of the original sheet, and ask them to write the name of any fruit on the paper. They are not to show you.

3. At the same time. hand one volunteer the other piece of paper which has two torn sides ad ask him to write down the name of a vegetable.

Try to be casual about which piece of paper you give to each volunteer, but ensure they get the "right" ones!

4. If you have enough members in the audience ask a fourth volunteer to come forward and place the three pieces of paper into the hat and mix them up.

5. Tell the audience you are able to pull out only the paper with the vegetable named on it. now reach into the hat, making a big deal out of the fact that you can't see the pieces of paper. Feel quickly for the piece of paper with two torn sides, and voilà! there is your vegetable!

Apple

CARROT

Banana

Hocus
Pocus

This trick will show you why mathematics is a magician's best friend! Remember it's best not to have to refer to a formila while performing, so memorize the sequence before you begin this trick.

You need: a set of dominoes and a calculator

1. Spread out the set of dominoes on the table and ask a volunteer to choose one. They should not let you see which one they choose.

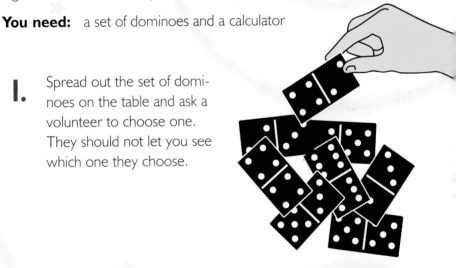

2. Now give them the calculator and ask them to do the following:
enter one of the domino's numbers
multiply that number by 5
add 7 to the total
double the new total
add the domino's other number to the result.

EG. domino 4
x5   = 20
+7   = 27
x2   = 54
+domino 2 = 56

3. Finally, ask your volunteer to hand the calculator to you with their answer still showing and say you are adding a bit of hocus pocus to find out which domino they chose.

4. As you showly say the magic words "Ho-cus po-cus" push in "-14=" on the calculator, which in the example above would give you an answer of 42-and of course 4 and 2 are the numbers on the chosen domino!

5. If the volunteer had begun their calculation by reversing the numbers (if he began the equation with 2 and added 4 later), the number on the calcualtor would be 24, as in 2 and 4.

WOW!